KU-213-161

Ways into Science

How Animals Move

Written by Peter Riley

W
FRANKLIN WATTS
LONDON•SYDNEY

Schools Library and Information Services

S00000654998

First published in 2003 by Franklin Watts
96 Leonard Street, London EC2A 4XD

Franklin Watts Australia
45-51 Huntley Street, Alexandria, NSW 2015

Copyright text © Peter Riley 2003
Copyright images © Franklin Watts 2003

Series editor: Sarah Peutrill
Art director: Jonathan Hair
Design: Ian Thompson
Photography: Ray Moller (unless otherwise credited)
Picture researcher: Diana Morris

A CIP catalogue record for this book is available from the
British Library

ISBN 0 7496 4740 X

Printed in Hong Kong/China

Picture Credits:
Ondrea Barbe/Corbis p. 22t; Jane Burton/Bruce Coleman Collection p. 7b; Philip
Colla/Ecoscene/Papilio p. 22b; Sarah Cook/Bruce Coleman Collection front cover t &
p. 15; Anthony Cooper/Ecoscene/Papilio p. 24b; Tim Davis/Corbis p. 21 © Dorling
Kindersely pp. 12b, 13t; Michael Fogden/Bruce Coleman Collection p. 23t; Brian
Knox/Ecoscene/Papilio front cover b & pp. 3, 20; Clarissa Leahy/Photofusion p. 18t;
Robert Maier/Bruce Coleman Collection p. 26c; Jack Milchanowski/Ecoscene/Papilio
p. 26cl; Natural Selection/Bruce Coleman Collection p. 6b; Pacific Stock/Bruce
Coleman Collection p. 7t; Robert Pickett/Ecoscene/Papilio pp. 19, 27tl; Alastair
Shay/Ecoscene/Papilio p. 24c; Barrie Watts p. 27tr; Jorge & Petra Wegner/Bruce
Coleman Collection p. 26bl

Whilst every attempt has been made to clear copyright should there be an
inadvertent omission please apply in the first instance to the publisher regarding
rectification.

Thanks to our models:
Donna Perkin, Nicholas Porter, Ayesha Selway,
Pernell Lamar Simpson

To my granddaughter Megan Kate

Contents

Different ways to move

Emily is walking.

This dog is running.

This bird
is flying.

These
fish are
swimming.

How many different ways
can you move?

Bones and muscles

Many animals have bones.

Bones hold the body together.

ribs

elbow

fingers

shin

Can you feel these bones?

8

Muscles pull on the bones to help you move.

Emily feels a muscle at the top of her arm.

Emily bends her arm. She can feel the muscle change to move the arm.

Try Emily's test.
How does your muscle change?

9

How do we walk?

Tom is walking very slowly.

He stands on one foot.

He can feel the muscles pulling.

He begins to lift his back foot.

Tom tips his body forwards. He feels his back foot push on the ground.

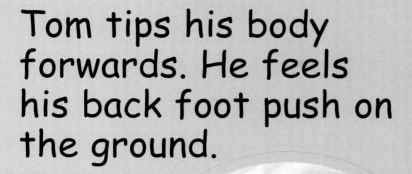

He puts his other foot down in front of him.

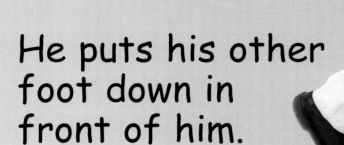

What does Tom do to keep walking?
Turn the page to find out.

Walking along

Tom puts his back foot in front of the other. Try this test to feel your muscles working.

When a dog takes one step, two legs move: the right front leg and the left back leg.

When a dog takes the next step,
the other two legs move.

Emily tries to move like
a walking dog. Can you?

Running

Running is faster than walking.

Harry is walking. One foot is always on the ground.

When he runs both feet leave the ground.

This cheetah is running.

It raises its front feet and pushes with its back feet.

For a few seconds all four feet leave the ground.

The cheetah brings its front feet down first.

Most animals with four legs run like this.

What is a **stride?**

The gap between footprints is called the stride.

Mia wants to find out if a stride is the same when people walk and run.

She walks across a sand pit.

She measures her stride.

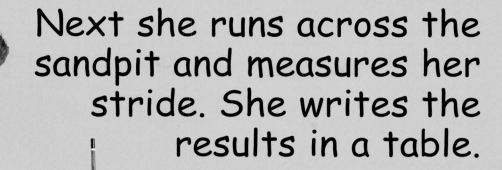

Next she runs across the sandpit and measures her stride. She writes the results in a table.

Mia asks four friends to do the test. Try Mia's test with your friends. Write your answers in a table.

Name	Walking stride	Running stride
1 Mia	14 cm	
2		
3		
4		
5		

What do your results show?

Crawling

When babies start to move about, they crawl.

Harry is crawling. He pushes with his hands and arms.

Can you crawl like a baby?

Some animals can crawl without arms or legs. Snails have special muscles that help them crawl.

The earthworm has tiny bristles to help it crawl. They stick in the soil to help it grip.

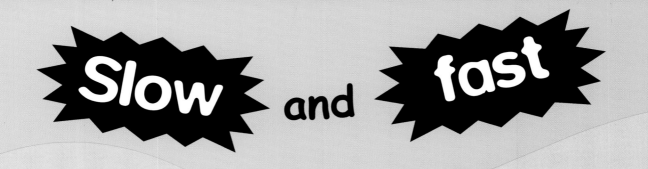 Slow and fast

Some animals move very slowly.

A large tortoise has a heavy
shell so it can only move slowly.

Many animals can move
fast and slow.

A chimp moves slowly up to other
chimps that are eating.

It moves
fast to
snatch
food from
them.

Can you move slowly then move
fast then move slowly again?

Swimming

Dan uses his arms and legs to swim.

A fish uses its fins to help it swim.

A seal has flippers to help it swim.

A frog has webbed feet. These help to push it through water.

Mia has a plastic bag over her hand to make it like a frog's foot.

She pushes her hand through water.

Try Mia's test with and without the bag. What difference does it make?

Flying

Wings push on air to make animals fly.

Many insects can fly.

Lots of birds fly too.

Tom has got two large pieces of card. He flaps them up and down like wings.

He feels the cards push on the air.

Try Tom's test. What can you feel?

How do they move?

Look at each animal and think about how many ways it can move.

26

Make a table like this. Put a tick in the columns to show how you think each animal can move.

animal	walk	run	crawl	swim	fly
bird				✓	
horse					
worm					
dog					
fish					
snail					

Useful words

bird – an animal with feathers and a pair of wings.

bone – an object inside the body which is made from a hard white material.

bristle – a short, tough hair.

cheetah – a kind of wild cat which can run very fast and lives on the plains in Africa.

chimp – a kind of ape which is really called a chimpanzee. It lives in Africa.

earthworm – a long thin animal with slimy skin and no legs.

elbow – the part that bends in the middle of an arm.

fish – an animal with fins and a skin covered in scales.

flipper – the part of the arm or leg of a seal which is shaped like a fin and helps it to swim.

insect – an animal with six legs. Most insects also have two or four wings.

muscle – one of the parts inside the body that makes movement.

ribs – the bones inside the chest.

shin – the bone at the front of the leg below the knee.

snail - an animal with a shell, and a long, fat body with feelers at one end.

spider – an animal with eight legs.

tortoise – a four-legged animal with a shell.

Some answers

Here are some answers to some of the questions we have asked in this book. Don't worry if you had some different answers to ours; you may be right, too. Talk through your answers with other people and see if you can explain why they are right.

Page 7   People can walk, run, hop, jump, crawl, roll around and swing on their arms on some kinds of playground equipment.

Page 9   The muscle becomes harder and shorter.

Page 17   You may find that your friends and you have different strides and the strides are bigger when you change from walking to running.

page 23   The bag does make a difference. The hand in the bag can push back more strongly than when the hand is pushed back with just the fingers spread apart.

Page 25   When the cards are flapped, the air can be felt pushing on them. It is this push of the air that lifts the bird upwards. When the wing pushes back, the air pushes the bird forwards.

Page 27   Fish – swim; Horse – walk, run, swim; Dog – walk, run, swim (sheepdogs also crawl); Snail – crawl; Bird – walk, run, fly (water birds, like the one shown, can also swim), Worm – crawl.

Index

About this book

Ways into Science is designed to encourage children to begin to think about their everyday world in a scientific way, examining cause and effect through close observation, recording their results and discussing what they have seen. Here are some pointers to gain the maximum use from **How Animals Move**.

• Working through this book will introduce the basic concepts about how animals move and also some of the language structures and vocabulary associated with movement (for example crawling, running and comparatives such as slow and fast). This will prepare the child for more formal work later in the school curriculum.

• On page 11, the children are invited to predict the result of a particular action. Ensure that you discuss the reason for any answer they give in some depth before turning over the page. In answering the question on page 11 look for an answer about moving the back foot to the front and to keep repeating this action to keep walking. You may like the children to copy Tom's activity on pages 10 and 11 before they make their prediction. When they have turned the page, let the children copy Tom's activity and feel their leg muscles. They may like to compare the muscle action with the action of arm muscles on page 9.

• Planning and making measurements are important activities in science and on pages 16 and 17 the children can see how Mia plans and carries out an investigation. You can use this activity to also test prediction skills as the children work through their own investigation on strides.

• On page 27 is a table for the children to copy and fill in using information they have found in the book and from their general knowledge. You may wish to spend some time talking with the children about the different possible ways in which animals may move.